MAE JEMISON

MAE JEMISON

Out of This World

CORINNE J. NADEN
and ROSE BLUE

A Gateway Biography
The Millbrook Press
Brookfield, Connecticut

Cover photograph courtesy of NASA

Photographs courtesy of NASA: pp. 13, 17, 21, 22, 23, 27, 34, 35; © Bettmann/Corbis: pp. 11, 18; AP/Wide World Photos: pp. 14, 20, 40; © Roger Ressmeyer/Corbis: pp. 6, 26, 28, 29, 31, 32; Stanford University News Service: p. 37

Library of Congress Cataloging-in-Publication Data
Naden, Corinne J.
Mae Jemison : out of this world / Corinne J. Naden and Rose Blue.
p. cm. — (Gateway biography)
Summary: Chronicles the life of Mae Jemison, an astronaut who became the first African-American woman in space.
Includes bibliographical references and index.
ISBN 0-7613-2570-0 (lib. bdg.)
1. Jemison, Mae, 1956—-Juvenile literature. 2. African American women astronauts—Biography—Juvenile literature. 3. Astronauts—United States—Biography—Juvenile literature. [1. Jemison, Mae, 1956- 2. Astronauts. 3. African Americans—Biography. 4. Women—Biography.] I. Blue, Rose. II. Title. III. Series.
TL789.85.J46 N33 2003
629.45'0092—dc21
2002000727

Published by The Millbrook Press, Inc.
2 Old New Milford Road
Brookfield, Connecticut 06804
www.millbrookpress.com

MAE JEMISON

Jemison's Dream

Some kids want to be doctors when they grow up. Some want to teach. Some just want to travel. Mae Jemison has done all three. She became a doctor and a teacher and she certainly has traveled. On September 12, 1992, she traveled right out of this world. That is, she flew into outer space. She was the first African-American woman in orbit. "When I was a little girl," she says, "I just wanted to know what was going on in the world. I was excited about everything around me. I looked at the stars, and I always assumed I'd go into space."

Mae Carol Jemison was born in Decatur, Alabama, on October 17, 1956. However, she calls Chicago her hometown because that's where she grew up. Her father, Charles, was a carpenter who worked at the United Charities of Chicago. Her mother, Dorothy, was a schoolteacher. Mae has two older siblings, Ada and Charles Jr. Their parents were very serious about providing them with a good education.

Even before high school, Jemison was hooked on space. She read all she could about Neil Armstrong and his landing on the Moon. She does not remember when she first dreamed of becoming an astronaut. She does know that "it has always been there."

By the time she was fourteen years old, Jemison was reading adult astronomy books. She spent a lot of time in Chicago's Museum of Science and Industry. She also spent time in art and dance classes and was on the school pom-pom squad. But little by little, she was becoming serious about space. In 1973 she graduated from Morgan Park High School with honors. She was just sixteen years old, but her mind was made up. She would follow a career in medicine and engineering. She hoped it would lead to space travel.

Jemison received a National Achievement Scholarship and entered Stanford University in California. She had two majors, chemical engineering and Afro-American studies. She also found time for dance, theater, and intramural football. She was the first female head of the Black Student Union. Science may be Jemison's main interest, but it is not her only one. She firmly believes in being what she calls an all-around person. "One's love for science doesn't get rid of all the other areas," she says.

On a New Path

When Jemison was about to graduate from Stanford in 1977, she heard that NASA (National Aeronautics and Space Administration) needed people for the space shuttle program. For a long time, NASA had recruited only white male pilots. Now it chose to include other people, especially scientists, women, and minorities. Jemison qualified on all three counts.

She thought long and hard about it. She knew she wanted to go into space. She knew that she might never again have the chance to apply for the program. But the time did not feel right to her. She decided to continue her education and hope for another chance.

With a bachelor of science degree she headed for Cornell University Medical College in New York City. By the time she earned her medical degree in 1981, the American Medical Student Association had sent her to other continents. She worked in rural Kenya in Africa, volunteering to give medical care to the villagers. Then she went to Thailand in Asia to offer medical care to refugees from Cambodia.

After Cornell, Jemison went to the Los Angeles County/University of Southern California Medical Center. In 1982 she opened her own doctor's office in Los Angeles.

Dr. Mae Jemison working in the medical office she opened in Los Angeles.

Still not ready to settle down, she joined the Peace Corps six months later. Jemison spent two and a half years in Sierra Leone and Liberia in West Africa. She was a doctor for Peace Corps volunteers and embassy workers.

Jemison felt that she learned a lot from the Peace Corps. She was one of the youngest doctors in her area and had to work hard to gain the respect of older people.

Bad Timing at NASA?

In 1985, when she was twenty-nine years old, Jemison returned to California. She worked for CIGNA Health Plans and took engineering courses at UCLA. Later that year she heard that NASA was seeking recruits once again. Now, the time was right.

Jemison's training and work experience gave her the confidence to apply for the astronaut program. She knew it was a long shot. Women were still new at NASA. American men had been in space for many years. John Glenn was the first American to orbit Earth in 1962. But it took twenty-one more years before Sally Ride became the first U.S. woman in space. African-American men had gone into space, but African-American women hadn't. But the times were changing.

Sally Ride, the first U.S. woman in space

Mae Jemison applied to NASA in 1985. She was one of two thousand who sent in applications.

In addition to bad odds, this was not a good time for *anybody* to try to enter the U.S. space program. The program suffered its most horrifying disaster only three

The Challenger *explosion in 1986 changed many people's attitude about the space program.*

months after Jemison sent her application to NASA. On January 28, 1986, the space shuttle *Challenger* took off from Cape Canaveral, Florida. There were five astronauts aboard, including Judy Resnick, the second woman in space, plus two civilians. One was school-teacher Christa McAuliffe.

Seventy-three seconds into the flight, the *Challenger* simply blew apart. It took two minutes and forty-five seconds to drop 65,000 feet (19,812 meters). The *Challenger* slammed into the Atlantic Ocean at a speed of 204 miles (328 kilometers) per hour. Everyone aboard was killed.

A great gloom settled over NASA and the nation. What had happened? Was this the end of the space program? Four months later, the government reported on the tragedy. It said that the *Challenger* exploded because a seal, called an O ring, had opened on the right rocket booster. The report said that the shuttle should not have been launched that morning. The weather was too cold.

NASA said that it would never forget the *Challenger* crew and reopened the program. In February 1987,

Jemison got a telephone call from Houston, Texas, where astronauts are trained. She did not have to be told. She was in.

NASA Training

After the phone call in February 1987, Jemison went to Houston for interviews. This included a background check and many physical and mental exams. The medical exam nearly ended her astronaut career before it began. They told her she had a heart murmur. Sometimes an abnormality in the heart causes a whooshing sound that a doctor can hear in addition to a heartbeat. That whooshing sound is called a murmur. Heart murmurs are not necessarily dangerous.

Jemison was discouraged. Could something that she thought was not serious keep her out of the space program? She informed NASA that it was discovered in medical school, but no one had been concerned about it. She was very relieved when they decided that it was not an issue.

SPACEFLIGHTS

America's spaceflights began in 1958 with the Mercury program. There were seven astronauts in the program, but the spacecraft carried only one passenger. The Mercury seven were all pilots and all men. They were said to have "the right stuff," meaning that they were brave enough and smart enough to fly in space.

After Mercury came Gemini. This was a bigger spacecraft for two astronauts. That program ended in 1966 after the astronauts walked in space.

Following Gemini was the big event, project Apollo. On July 16, 1969, Commander Neil Armstrong and astronauts Edwin Aldrin Jr. and Michael Collins lifted off from Kennedy Space Center at 9:32 A.M. On July 20, the lunar module, which detached from the spacecraft, settled down on the Moon's surface. The whole world watched. At 10:56 P.M., Neil Armstrong became the first person to step on the Moon. After that, five more Apollo flights landed on the Moon. The program ended in 1972. There haven't been any Moon landings since then.

Following Apollo came four missions of the Skylab space station, from 1973 to 1974. Then the Apollo-Soyez Test Project (ASTP) took place in 1975. American and Russian crews docked their vehicles in space. After that, NASA began its current space shuttle program. The first shuttle flight was in 1981.

Neil Armstrong walking on the Moon

Mae Jemison is interviewed soon after she finds out she has been accepted into NASA's astronaut program. She told reporters: "I'm not afraid of being in the program. I have confidence that what things can be done to correct problems have been done and NASA will continue to work to achieve a good safety record."

Jemison went back to California and waited. The next call came on June 4. She was one of fifteen selected to be an astronaut candidate. She was the first African-American woman.

Why was Mae Jemison chosen for the astronaut candidate program? Why did NASA decide that she had "the right stuff"? Back in 1959 when the first astronauts were picked, they had to be jet pilots no more than 5 feet 11 inches (180 centimeters) tall. This was because the space capsule was so small. Now an astronaut can be as tall as 6 feet 4 inches (193 centimeters).

As time went on, NASA began to concentrate more on high quality education than flight experience. By the time Jemison applied, candidates were judged on academics alone. Jemison was no jet pilot, but she certainly had a good education.

Yet, Jemison's dream was still at least a year away. Astronaut candidates must spend a year in training at the Johnson Space Center in Houston. After training they might be selected for space shuttle missions. Becoming a candidate, though, does not mean becoming an astronaut. Those selected at the end of the first year will remain with NASA for another five years.

So, Mae Jemison went back to school once again. This school was like no other she had experienced. For one year at the Johnson Space Center in Houston, Jemison took classes in the shuttle system, geology, meteorology, mathematics, oceanography, astronomy, physics, and other related subjects. She

Jemison sits in the commander's seat aboard a replica space shuttle during her training in 1987.

The Johnson Space Center in Houston, Texas, where Mae trained to be an astronaut

was trained in parachute jumping, scuba diving, and how to survive on land and sea. She experienced periods of weightlessness such as those she would encounter in space. She also had to fly a jet plane at least four hours a month because she was training to become a mission specialist.

THE SPACE SHUTTLE

The space shuttle is a reusable space vehicle. It can carry seven people. The shuttle is designed to transport people and scientific gear, such as huge cameras or computers, to and from Earth. The space shuttle has three major parts.

The *orbiter* is about the size and shape of a DC-9 jet with three main engines. It is designed to last for about one hundred missions. It is both home and workplace for the crew. The orbiter blasts off into space, but lands like a conventional airplane with the help of a huge drag chute. If the orbiter has to land other than at the Kennedy Space Center from where it blasted off, it may be carried home piggyback on a huge shuttle carrier aircraft.

The orbiter lands like an airplane with the help of a drag chute that trails behind.

The three major parts of the space shuttle: The orbiter has the NASA logo and the American flag on its wings; the rust-colored external tank sits in between the two solid rocket boosters.

The *external tank* holds liquid hydrogen and oxygen for the orbiter's engines. This is the only shuttle part that is not reused. Two *solid rocket boosters (SRBs)* burn with the orbiter's engines on liftoff. They are recovered and used for about twenty missions.

An astronaut can join a space shuttle crew in one of three positions: commander/pilot, mission specialist, or payload specialist. The commander is responsible for the entire mission and everyone on board. The pilot helps to control and operate the space vehicle. The mission specialist operates experiments in space and takes space walks. Pay-load specialists are not NASA astronauts. They may be citizens of another country or, in the case of teacher Christa McAuliffe aboard the *Challenger*, someone with a special job for a certain flight. All astronauts must meet similar requirements of education and experience. The commander/pilot, however, must have at least one thousand hours of experience in jet planes.

Out of This World

At last, the training period was over. It was August 1988. Jemison had made it. She was a mission specialist astronaut. Now she could be assigned to a shuttle mission.

The future turned out to be a five-year wait. During that time, astronaut Jemison lived and worked at the Johnson Space Center. She also worked on her doctorate of science degree, which she received from Lincoln University in 1991.

During this period, Jemison kept in touch with her family and saw them whenever she could. Her father and mother, who are now deceased, always encouraged her space dreams. So did her sister and brother. Meanwhile, Ada Jemison Bullock became a doctor and Charles Jr. entered the real estate business.

Finally, Jemison was assigned to a mission. It was STS-47 Spacelab J, scheduled for blastoff in September 1992. This was the fiftieth space shuttle flight. The mission commander was Robert L. Gibson. Among the six-person crew were three "firsts." Jemison was the first African-American woman in space. Mark Lee, the payload commander, and Jan Davis, mission specialist, were the first married couple in space. And Mamoru Mohri from NASDA (National Space Development Agency) in Japan was the first citizen of that country to fly in the shuttle.

THOSE BULKY SPACE SUITS

As an astronaut, Mae Jemison had to learn to live in a space suit. These bulky outfits are what allow people to exist and work in space. Inside the space shuttle, astronauts can work in flight suits or slacks and short-sleeved shirts. But there is no oxygen in space. So outside the shuttle, they must carry their environment around with them in the space suit. It protects against extreme cold and extreme heat in outer space, and it protects against being smacked by a flying space rock. (Lots of big and small particles fly about in outer space.)

The largest space suit includes its own system for air conditioning, method of talking with the spacecraft, and device for collecting urine. It contains a helmet and visor, a drink bag, and more. It weighs 107 pounds (49 kg) and costs millions of dollars. Space suits must be cleaned and dried after each flight, and they last about eight years.

Astronauts must always inspect their space suits to make sure each component works correctly.

Before the launch, astronaut Jemison was asked if she was nervous about going into space, or if she thought about the *Challenger* disaster. She said no. She knew she was sitting on dangerous explosives during blastoff. But she said that everyone knew what he or she was supposed to do. She trusted the people she worked with. "If you keep worrying about it," she said, "you're not going to be able to do your job."

Jemison reviews some of her responsibilities as a mission specialist at the Kennedy Space Center soon before blastoff in September 1992.

The launch of the *Endeavour* from the Kennedy Space Center was right on time—10:23 A.M., September 12, 1992. During her eight days of space time, Jemison helped to conduct some forty-three scientific experiments. Some concerned the effects of weightlessness and the loss of calcium.

Jemison and the rest of the crew are on their way to the Endeavour. *In front (left to right) are Curtis Brown, Jay Apt, and Robert Gibson; behind them are Jan Davis and Mark Lee; and in the rear are Mamoru Mohri and Mae Jemison.*

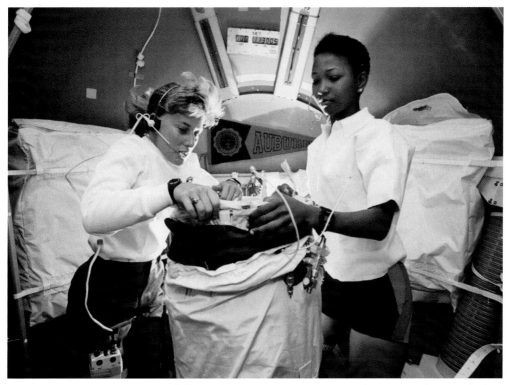

Jemison and Davis set up an experiment aboard the Endeavour. *They performed many experiments in space.*

Calcium is the chief element in human bones and teeth. As people—especially women—age, their bones tend to lose some calcium. This loss of calcium in bones is called *osteoporosis*. In space, everyone loses calcium. Women lose even more the longer they stay up there. Jemison's experiments were concerned with this loss and how to keep people healthy.

Another experiment studied motion sickness and the use of biofeedback. Jemison did not take medicine to prevent motion sickness in space, but many astronauts do. It is common for them to feel sick during the first days in space. But sometimes taking medicine for motion sickness has side effects that prevent an astronaut from working. Biofeedback is a type of mental training that allows a person to control problems such as motion sickness without taking medicine.

In addition, Jemison tried to find out how weightlessness affects humans and animals. For instance, would tadpoles in space develop into frogs just as they do on Earth? Jemison observed tadpoles on the mission. She eventually claimed that the tadpoles were "right on track." They turned into healthy frogs just as they were supposed to.

After 127 orbits, the *Endeavour* returned to Kennedy. Mae Jemison had successfully become the first African-American woman in space. She logged 190 space hours. When asked what spaceflight felt like,

Some of the crew members working, and playing, while onboard the Endeavour. *Jemison said she felt very free while floating in space.*

she told Oprah Winfrey in a TV interview in April 2001: "You could float . . . it was like you were in a huge pool of water . . . this incredible sense of freedom. . . . For me, it was the most incredible sensation. . . . I was doing exactly what I wanted to, and I thought about that little girl who used to dream of the stars."

Lots of people asked more practical things. What did Jemison eat in space? Although the space shuttle

Jemison and Davis eat aboard the Endeavour. *Jemison later said the food really wasn't all that bad.*

will probably never be mistaken for a first-class restaurant, Jemison said it was really not so bad. In the past, the crews ate meals from containers by adding water and kneading the mixture by hand. But for larger crews on a week or more mission such as Jemison's, a mission kit is loaded on the mid deck of the orbiter. It has special serving trays and an oven to warm the food packages. There is even a small dining area with a table and foot stirrups. Astronauts have to anchor themselves while eating or they may float to the ceiling along with their ham and cheese sandwich!

Typical meals for one day aboard the shuttle might be orange juice, scrambled eggs, sausage, and coffee for breakfast; soup, sandwich, banana, and cookies for lunch; and shrimp cocktail, steak, broccoli, strawberries, and cocoa for dinner. Scientists think that one day astronauts may grow their own vegetable gardens in space.

How did Jemison keep clean in space? Sanitation is very important in such a confined space with a lack of gravity. Infections could spread easily to everyone on

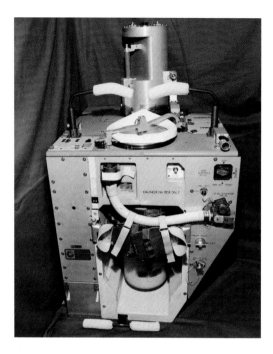

The Waste Collection System, or toilet, of a space shuttle

board. Since there is no washing machine, when clothes are changed—such as socks or underwear every two days—they must be sealed in plastic bags. There is no shower either so only sponge baths are possible. The water comes from a device that looks like a handgun. Bathroom facilities operate very much like those on Earth.

Astronaut Jemison is lucky that she did not have to shave. Male astronauts have a problem with shaving. When cut, the whiskers are apt to float about the shuttle and get into the equipment.

THE INTERNATIONAL SPACE STATION

All of the data collected so far, from Jemison's spaceflight and those
before and after it, have come together in the most complicated scientific
project ever. It is the International Space Station, begun in 1998 with the
launch of the Unity and Zarya modules from the United States and Russia.
Fourteen other nations are involved as well. This space complex is
huge—it is nearly as long as three football fields. The research conducted
in its six laboratories may lead to discoveries in medicine and science that
will help people all over the world.

Jemison was much in the spotlight after her return to Earth. She was interviewed on television and radio. Her hometown of Chicago staged many celebrations. Jemison visited her old high school. She encouraged young people, especially young women, to follow their dreams.

Many awards followed, including several honorary doctorates. She was given the Ebony Black Achievement Award in 1992. An alternative public school in Detroit, Michigan, was named in her honor. In 1993 she was even inducted into the National Women's Hall of Fame in Seneca Falls, New York. That same year she made a guest appearance on the TV program *Star Trek: The Next Generation*. *People* magazine also named her one of the "50 Most Beautiful People in the World."

During her talks, Jemison spoke of many things besides spaceflight. She calls herself a "womanist." She has strong feelings that women must take responsibility for their lives. She urges more women to get

Jemison was the 1996 commencement speaker at Stanford University. She advised graduates never to be afraid of failure.

involved in the space program: "It is our right," she says. And that especially includes black women. "Space belongs to all of us," Jemison declared, "not to any one group. . . . "

What Now, Astronaut?

In the year after her first spaceflight, Mae Jemison retired from NASA. She had been with the program for six years. She said later that she would have liked to have been part of later missions, such as the International Space Station. But that would have meant waiting another eight or nine years for the chance. And there was so much else she wanted to do.

Dartmouth College invited Jemison to their Hanover, New Hampshire, campus to teach a course in its environmental studies program. She is currently a member of the Dartmouth faculty.

Jemison has always been concerned with science and technology and how it affects human life. To deal with these concerns, she formed The Jemison Group, Inc. It is based in Houston, where Jemison now lives with her two cats, Sneeze and Little Mama.

The company designs and develops technical and communication systems especially for underdeveloped countries. It organized "The Earth We Share" program, an international science camp for twelve- to sixteen-year-olds. This was prompted by Jemison's concern about overpopulation in the world. It invites teenagers to solve problems using science and technology.

Jemison is also busy lecturing around the country. Her speeches involve ways in which science and tech-

A NONPROFIT ORGANIZATION

In 1994, Jemison started a nonprofit organization named for her mother. It is called The Dorothy Jemison Foundation for Excellence. Its goal is to develop teaching materials and programs so that young people will grow up prepared to contribute to society. Dorothy Jemison was part of the public school system for twenty-five years.

Jemison receives an honorary Doctor of Science degree at the Rutgers University graduation ceremonies in May 2001.

nology can improve the quality of human life. She speaks as someone who has seen the beauty of Earth from outer space. She is very concerned about maintaining that beauty. This involves protecting our natural resources, such as keeping our water supplies clean and making sure that we put aside land for trees to grow.

When Jemison is asked what made her so successful, she says she owes her good fortune to her teachers and her parents. They always supported her dreams and ambitions. They also encouraged her to question things and explore on her own. She thinks too many kids today are told what to do or what not to do. "It's important that we start recognizing that every individual in society has skills and talents," she says.

She remembers one day when she was in kindergarten and was asked the usual question, "What do you want to be when you grow up?" She said "scientist." The teacher asked, "Don't you mean nurse?" Jemison replied no, she meant "scientist." As she says, there is nothing wrong with being a nurse, but that was not what she meant.

Mae Jemison has fulfilled her dream of becoming an astronaut. She is working on her dream of making the world a better place in which to live. But is once an astronaut, always an astronaut? Is this veteran of the outer limits still interested in space? As she said in an interview, "I'd go to Mars at the drop of a hat."

TIMELINE

1956   Mae Jemison is born on October 17; shortly after, the family moves to Chicago.

1973   Graduates from Morgan Park High School, Chicago.

1977   Graduates from Stanford University with a bachelor of science in chemical engineering; enters Cornell University Medical College, New York City; does volunteer medical work in Africa and Asia.

1981   Earns medical degree from Cornell.

1982   Enters private practice in Los Angeles; joins Peace Corps in Africa.

1985   Joins CIGNA in California; applies to NASA space program in October.

1987   Accepted into space program in June.

1992   First spaceflight, September 12, as part of the crew of *Endeavour*; wins Ebony Black Achievement award.

1993   Wins Montgomery Fellowship from Dartmouth College, where she accepts teaching position; enters National Women's Hall of Fame; named one of the "50 Most Beautiful People in the World" by *People* magazine; founds The Jemison Group, Inc.; makes her home in Houston, Texas.

1994   Establishes The Dorothy Jemison Foundation for Excellence in honor of her mother.

2002   Lives in Houston with her two cats and is a member of the Dartmouth faculty and director of The Jemison Group.

FOR MORE INFORMATION

Books

Canizares, Susan, and Samantha Berger. *The Voyage of Mae Jemison.* New York: Scholastic, 1999.

Gelletly, LeeAnne. *Mae Jemison.* Philadelphia: Chelsea, 2001.

Jemison, Mae. *Find Where the Wind Goes: Moments From My Life.* New York: Scholastic, 2001.

Yannuzzi, Della A. *Mae Jemison: A Space Biography.* New York: Enslow, 1998.

Web Sites

Dr. Mae Jemison's Official Home Page
    www.maejemison.com

How Space Suits Work
    www.howstuffworks.com/space-suit9.htm

NASA Human Spaceflight
    www.spaceflight.nasa.gov.station

NASA SpaceLink
    http://spacelink.nasa.gov/

WORKS CONSULTED

"America's Spaceport: John F. Kennedy Space Center," NASA.

"Countdown! NASA Space Shuttles and Facilities," NASA, Sept 2000.

"Dr. Mae Jemison," http://quest.arc.nasa.gov/women/TODTWD/jemison.bio.html

Green, Constance M. "To Boldly Go," *Ms.* magazine, July/Aug 1992.

Jemison, Mae. *Find Where the Wind Goes: Moments From My Life.* New York: Scholastic, 2001.

La Blanc, Michael L., ed. "Mae C. Jemison." *Contemporary Black Biography*, Vol. 1. Detroit: Gale Group, 1992.

"Living and Working on the New Frontier," NASA, Sept 1994.

Mabunda, L., ed. "Mae C. Jemison." *African-American Almanac*, 7th ed. Detroit: Gale Group, 1997.

"NASA Facts: Astronaut Selection and Training," NASA, Aug 1993.

"1981–1999 Space Shuttle Mission Chronology," NASA.

"Oprah," The Oprah Winfrey Show, April 12, 2001.

INDEX